COSTUME OF THE WESTERN WORLD

ELIZABETHAN AND JACOBEAN
1558—1625

COSTUME OF THE WESTERN WORLD

Edited by James Laver

THE TUDORS TO LOUIS XIII

Each uniform with this book
With 8 Plates in Colour
and Many in Monochrome

COSTUME OF THE WESTERN WORLD

ELIZABETHAN AND JACOBEAN
1558–1625

by

GRAHAM REYNOLDS

Deputy Keeper Department of Paintings
Victoria and Albert Museum

GEORGE G. HARRAP AND COMPANY LTD
LONDON SYDNEY TORONTO BOMBAY

First published 1951
by GEORGE G. HARRAP & CO. LTD
182 High Holborn, London, W.C. 1
Copyright. All rights reserved

*This edition is not to be sold in
the United States of America or its
Dependencies.*

Intercontinental Publishing Company, Amsterdam
Text printed by H. Veenman & Zonen, Wageningen
Colour and monochrome plates printed by Vada, Wageningen
Printed in the Netherlands

ELIZABETHAN AND JACOBEAN

1558–1625

THE RENAISSANCE, after more than one false start, came ultimately to England in the Elizabethan Age. It came as a belated recognition of spiritual forces which had been active on the Continent for over a century, and because it came late it came in full flood. Men abandoned themselves to the new fullness in learning and life with a zest which revealed how austere had been their deprivation throughout the long Gothic twilight. Here, as it had elsewhere, the revivifying enthusiasm penetrated all the spheres of human activity: the scholar composing his system of pedagogics, the states-man drafting his political memoranda, was caught up in it, no less than the craftsman making his designs to a new pattern. Into whatever feature of the late sixteenth century in England we may inquire we are conscious of a sense of new ideas in the air; of vitality and strength. In literature this ferment brought forth something of more than merely ephemeral or national interest. In the visual arts, however, a deficiency of training and tradition meant that the creative energy was sometimes misdirected and ill-applied; too often it spent itself in a display of badly assimilated learning, in an ostentation of ornament and decoration derived at second or third hand from antique sources. Visually, indeed, the England of Elizabethan times is like a child, with a child's vitality, a child's delight in bright colours, and a child's desire to fill all of a blank surface with a simple, easily repeated pattern.

Costume is one of the expressions of the visual sensibility of an age, and through its very universality the impress of the English Renaissance is to be discerned also in the subject of this short study. The dress of the Elizabethan Age, and of the Jacobean Age which was its somewhat rueful appendage, bears all the differentiating marks of con-temporary English design; it is luxurious almost to excess, but the sense of harmony in form which it displays is unsure, ornament proliferates over it in abundance, and the striving for originality often produces bizarre results. It borrows much from Conti-nental sources—its main lines from Spain, elaborations from France and Italy; but as they cross the Channel these elements are transmuted, and a purely insular style derives from them. It is a style which truthfully reflects the national spirit—one of bravery, bravado, and swashbuckling, of supreme confidence and even arrogance in a newly discovered strength.

The mainspring of the Renaissance was the imitation of classical models, but the Renaissance spirit in costume is to be found in these inward parallels rather than in its

5

actual exterior. Direct emulations of antique dress were to be seen in theatrical costume and the costumes for masques; but it was left for the Revolutionary era in France to apply strictly classical principles to the wear of everyday life. The Elizabethans were content to take the doublet and hose they knew and to transform them, rather than to assume the toga, though there might be found in the designs of embroidery and patterns of lace an echo of antique decorative motifs. They showed also their liking for erudition by lending their costumes to a display of colour symbolism. A lover would wear a blue favour to testify to his truth of heart, and his mistress would answer him by putting on a green bow to show that she rejoiced in his service. The armillary sphere and the knots on Sir Henry Lee's shirt (Plate 4), no less than the sun, moon, and stars on Richard Sackville's trunk hose (Plate 33), are emblems charged with a similar allusiveness, but they speak a dead language to us now. A more transparent symbolism was displayed by Mary, Queen of Scots, when at her execution she doffed her outer garments of black and was seen to be clothed entirely in red; it was a gesture worthy of the age.

As we look more closely into our period we can discern a difference of temper between its Elizabethan and Jacobean components, a difference which corresponds with that in the poetry and drama of those two contrasting epochs. For all their extravagance, there is something vernal about Elizabethan clothes, in their colour, their cut, and the air with which they are worn; their fresh, spring-like glow answers to the lyricism of Spenser's poems and Shakespeare's earlier plays. Almost directly upon the accession of James I a note of restraint is to be discerned: the taste shown in dress is even improved, but it is the improvement of sophistication. The harmony of white and gold is replaced by that of orange and bay-green; the colours of dress become the secondary ones, reflecting more complicated emotions. The youth has aged, and we are in the grown-up world of the tragedies of Shakespeare and Webster, a world of disillusionment and heartsearching.

The literature of the time is full of allusions to costume; excesses were lashed by the satirists, such as Stubbes, and it provided many a theme for comedy. But though these literary references supply an index of social usages and a glossary of the words used for naming different portions of costume and different styles of fashion—a glossary which it is now often difficult to interpret—they do not by themselves build up a coherent picture of the vesture of the age. Fortunately the national delight in portrait-painting was as strong in the Elizabethan and Jacobean Ages as it has been ever since in England, and it was served by an adequate if not outstanding body of visiting artists. More fortunately still, it was the custom throughout this period for the painter to inscribe his canvas with the sitter's age and the year of the portrait. The majority of the illustrations which are provided here to present a survey of the pattern of change running through the costume of the Elizabethan and Jacobean Ages are taken from these dated portraits, or from dated miniatures out of the more delectable national contribution to its portraiture. In these portraits the costume is as much to the fore as the features of the sitter; the clothes represent his personal choice and are as sensitive an index as his physiognomy to his character.

Because the fashion of a given period is an organic growth we can really understand it only in the study of its changes. The Ditchley portrait of Queen Elizabeth (Plate 25) does, it is true, tell us all we need to know about the Court style of 1592; but it tells much more when compared with the costume of the Queen in 1585 (Plate 17) and of Queen Anne of Denmark in 1617 (Plate 38). These comparisons actualize the tensions which were felt in the age itself, at the waist-line, at the neck, in the sleeves, and in the skirt, the tensions of which the tailors were themselves aware as the fashion altered one or more of these details year by year, and which, in the literal sense of Hamlet's words, "show . . . the very age and body of the time his form and pressure."

In fact, in this period more than in any other, the shape of the clothed human body was as clay in the hands of the tailors; with wire and bombast they compressed it here and inflated it there, regardless of the anatomical structure of legs and arms, of waists and bosoms. At times they produced results so different from the natural human form that one is forcibly reminded of the deformations and mutilations practised upon themselves by savage tribes. This is particularly the case in the closing decade of the reign of Queen Elizabeth, when the bodice was restricted to a narrow inverted cone standing on its point upon the enormous cylinder of the drum farthingale, flanked at the sides by puffed leg-of-mutton sleeves and crowned by a great ruff (Plate 25). But the steps to this idiosyncratic style, and those which led from it, displayed more sense of equilibrium.

The basic components of dress for men and women remained unchanged throughout the Elizabethan and Jacobean Ages. The fundamental garments for men were, as they had been for over a century, and were to remain till the second half of the seventeenth century, the doublet and hose.

The doublet was a thick, quilted upper garment, of velvet, silk, satin, leather, or other material, which extended from the neck to below the waist. It fitted close to the body, buttoning up the middle, but was generally shaped on artificially induced lines, and for almost the whole of the Elizabethan Age had a more or less pronounced peascod form. For most of the period it was constructed with a high neck, and flared out below the waist into shorter or longer skirts; in fact, the length of these skirts or tabs below the waist is one of the features which show most variation. The sleeves were sometimes detachable, and could be made of different material from the body of the doublet. The points where the sleeves met the body of the doublet were given a decorative treatment and were known as the 'wings.' Outliving their original purpose of making an ornamental feature of the row of ribbons tying the sleeve to the body of the doublet, these survived into the time when the doublet was made of one piece and became flat, broad ridges of material. The body of the doublet was decorated by one or more of a number of favourite expedients; for instance, by embroidery, by an embossed pattern, or by pinking or slashing whereby an under-lining, possibly of different colour, might be exposed. When slashing was adopted it might take the form of short, diagonal cuts or longer, vertical incisions which formed narrow panels of material known as 'panes.' A jerkin, closely fitting to the same form as the doublet and with or without sleeves, was often worn over it.

The hose covered the lower part of a man's body from the waist to the feet. Throughout the Elizabethan and Jacobean period they were formed of two parts—the breeches, more or less short and shaped away from the body, and the 'nether stocks,' which correspond to our stockings, fitting closely to the leg and over the knee like tights. Despite this clear division of their form, hose were sometimes made in one piece; but there was a growing tendency for them to be divided into their two obvious parts. Much invention was lavished on the breeches, and a number of types are mentioned by name in the literature of the time under the titles of 'trunk hose,' 'Venetians,' 'canions,' 'galligaskins,' 'slops,' and so forth. It is not so easy in practice to identify each of these designations with the variations known to us in illustration. It may be taken, however, that trunk hose, round-shaped, stuffed, cut in panes, and worn halfway down the thigh, are the characteristic breeches of the Elizabethan Age; at one period, however, they reach to little below the hips. Canions appear to be the telescopelike, closely fitting extensions which link short trunk hose to the nether stocks (shown in Plate 19). Venetians are a variant of trunk hose, often tight-fitting, but differentiated by their reaching below the knee, as worn by the young James I in Plate 11. The shaped breeches were padded with a substance known as 'bombast,' composed of flock, rags, or any other serviceable stuff. The hose were in the earlier part of our period attached to the doublet by laces or 'points,' which were brought through a line of eyelet holes at the waistline itself and tied visibly in front with gay and decorative ribbons. Later they were fastened by means of hooks and eyes to a false skirt underneath, and the points formerly used for fastening became a hanging decorative fringe.

The outermost garment in a man's suit of clothes was either a gown or a cloak. The gown reached to the ground, was customarily enriched with fur sleeves, and was the perquisite of older men, members of the professions, or the middle classes in more ceremonious attire. It is, for example, worn by the graver guests at the *Marriage Feast at Bermondsey* (Plate 8). The fashionable wear for young men and courtiers was the cloak, extending only to half-length, and worn with an air over the left shoulder only, as, for instance, by the young man in Hilliard's miniature who is leaning against a tree among roses and thinking of his mistress (Plate 18). In this case the cloak has a hanging cowl, but in another style it might have a collar standing up stiffly from the shoulders. Wearing a cloak out of doors was evidently regarded as an indispensable attribute of gentility, for we read of men who are compared to tapsters for running up and down without their cloaks.

Two sorts of hat were popular—the low-crowned hat of soft material, decorated with a feather (as in Plate 11), and the high-crowned hat made of stiffened material and of sugar-loaf form. As is apparent from the frequency of combat in the literature and chronicles of the age, swords were a conspicious concomitant to civilian clothes, and were attached to the man's girdle by a hanger (see Plates 24 and 31). In coiffure men were fairly evenly divided between the choice of short pointed beard with a moustache, or cleanshavenness. A dandiacal idiosyncrasy introduced about 1590 was the love lock— a lock of hair on the left-hand side allowed to grow long and full over the collar. This mode was adopted by Henry Wriothesley, Earl of Southampton, Shakespeare's patron, and was continued into the following century and the age of Van Dyck.

The fundamental garment in the woman's wardrobe was known as the kirtle; and this was often composed of the two separate parts which go to make up its form—the bodice and the skirt. For most of the period under review these two elements of the kirtle have emphatically contrasting forms, the bodice tapering to a sharp point at or below the waistline, while the skirt is in the shape of an upright cone, bell, or drum. The skirt derived its form from the device known as the farthingale. The farthingale was originally an importation from Spain, and then consisted of a petticoat stiffened with hoops. For almost the whole of our period, however, the *Spanish* farthingale over a framework existed side by side with the *French* farthingale. The latter acquired its characteristic form by the use of a padded roll fitted like a motor-tyre round the hips. It is not always possible to tell from the inspection of a portrait whether the farthingale owes its form to a stiff framework or a padded petticoat. The drum farthingale, a third form, characteristic of the last years of Queen Elizabeth's reign (Plates 25 and 30), clearly depends upon a hoop at waist-level.

The farthingale is as characteristic of Elizabethan and Jacobean costume as the ruff, and gives rise to as much satire and obloquy. For instance, Bosola says in *The Duchess of Malfi*:

> A whirlwind strike off these bawd farthingales!
> For, but for that and the loose-bodied gown,
> I should have discovered apparently
> The young springal cutting a caper in her belly.

The theory that the farthingale was invented to conceal the misdemeanours of a Spanish princess is presumed to be one of the legends which invariably spring up to account for the more surprising elements of fashion, but it is certainly true that the device was known as *cache-enfant* in the sixteenth century. When it went out of fashion in the middle of the seventeenth century the farthingale became a laughable symbol of the old-fashioned. But the graveyard of past modes has never failed to provide suggestions for the fashions of later ages, and the farthingale was resuscitated, with more graceful articulation with the bodice, in the hooped skirts worn by women for the greater part of the eighteenth century, and in the crinoline of the mid-nineteenth century. In Elizabethan times the skirt might be parted in front in an inverted V form, either to reveal an elaborately ornamented petticoat or to receive a detachable panel of embroidery, which fitted into the gap. These panels could be used, of course, to provide all manner of contrasts with the material of the kirtle. The way in which

9

they were attached by bows to the skirt is explained almost diagrammatically by Plate 16.

The bodice was constricted to its artificial shape by busks, stays, and even iron bodies. It entered into its varying waistline with a sharp point until almost the end of our period. Far more consistently than in the male doublet, the sleeves of the bodice were separate entities, often of different colour and material, and they went through many forms, from the close-fitting cylinders of the 1560's to the puffed, slashed, and wired-out leg-of-mutton sleeves of the 1580's. The wings, or points of junction of sleeve and bodice, become of great decorative significance in an intermediate phase between these two styles; they are puffed and paned with strips of contrasting material, and form one of the chief points of interest of the whole costume, in particular providing a squareness of shoulder which is not otherwise to be seen in the dress of this century. At the time this style held sway the bodice was cut low and square at the top, and it was the custom to cover the bosom with a 'partlet' of gauze or other semi-transparent material, which was often embroidered with black work. Subsequently it became the practice for unmarried women to leave this area bare: Elizabeth, as the Virgin Queen, followed this custom during the last years of her reign, and *décolletage* became more general in the reign of James I.

A gown was sometimes worn over the kirtle; when this was so, it usually fell entirely to the back of the body. In its more extreme form it degenerated into a pair of false sleeves attached to the back of the bodice, as in the Ditchley portrait of Queen Elizabeth (Plate 25).

The characteristic headdresses of the age are the coif and the French hood. The coif, of embroidered linen, network, or other material, covered the back of the head, and little of it is to be seen in portraits with a frontal posture, except possibly the frill at its edge (Plate 44). The French hood also confined the hair on the back of the head, but was of stiffened material and hung down in a veil which reached below the ruff (Plate 42); the hanging veil might, however, be drawn up and pinned to the crown of the hood, or wired into wing-shaped extensions behind the head and shoulders. An outburst of masculinity about 1590 led to the imitation of men's high hats in women's headgear; but thereafter it became more common for the hair to be uncovered. The hair itself, visible only in a thin strip between the front of the headdress and the forehead, was at first parted in the middle. With the advance of the 1570's and 1580's it was curled and wired out to either side in a horn-shaped figure (Plate 43), the width getting larger step by step with the ruffs and the puffed sleeves. After 1590 this horn-shaped coiffure gives way to one which rises vertically from the forehead, and by 1600 curls are superseded by hair brushed flat and shaped high over a pad (Plate 52). At about this time and later some ladies, perhaps mainly unmarried ones, adopted the delightfully romantic style of long hair falling loosely over their shoulders (Plate 53). The hair is bedecked with jewels, often wired into delicate cresting.

Jewels, indeed, whether real or imitation, make a prominent contribution to the

10

colour of Court costume. Queen Elizabeth wore pearls, rubies, and diamonds and other stones in her hair, pendant from her ears, in her ruffs, in elaborate necklaces, lockets, and rings, and was followed, with slightly less ostentation, by the ladies of her Court. The Queen's first wearing of silk stockings in 1560, after which she would wear none of cloth, is recorded in contemporary chronicles, and her doeskin gloves with their embroidered tabs were sweetly perfumed.

For the first half of our period shoes were heelless and decorated by a simple form of slashing. Heels came in during the reign of James I (see Plates 33 and 35), and the large rosette at the buckle became the favourite method of ornament. Among the other incidentals to costume may be included the fan, in which, again, there are contrasting usages in the two halves of the period. Feather fans on a fixed handle were used up to about 1590; thereafter they gave way to the folding fans which became popular through the expansion of trade with the Far East.

But the most remarkable feature of both male and female costume is to be found in its neckwear, and particularly in the ruff. This provides a standard example of the tendency of all abnormalities in costume to begin with a slight exaggeration, which rapidly gathers way until it advances to an extreme. This law had already been exemplified by the pointed toes of the end of the fourteenth century and the towering headdresses worn by women in the second half of the fifteenth century. The modest beginnings of the ruff, as a frill at the neck and sleeves of the shirt or shift, is exemplified in the illustrations of costume before 1570. The tendency to extravagance in the splendour of this feature seems at first to have been confined to the adornment of its edges by embroidery. But already by 1570 it had increased in depth of pleating and joined up all round the neck, instead of leaving a gap for the chin. Thereafter its growth and elaboration were uninterrupted. It became a separate article of attire; the introduction of starch into England in 1564 had enabled it to be extended away from the neck in all the convolutions of its pleating. At the same time as it extended in breadth and length, it provided scope for the display of the most elaborate geometrical tracery possible to reticella lace (Plates 43 and 44). Persons of slightly less social pretension or less deep purses might wear ruffs as broad and serpentine, but without this lacework. The limits of this development of the ruff outward—imposed, no doubt, by the refusal of the material to respond to further width—was reached about 1585 in the cartwheel ruff (Plates 17, 43, and 44).

At the very height of this extreme, and concurrently with it, some fashionable men, no doubt the apostles of a new simplicity, abandoned the ruff entirely in favour of the falling collar; but the simplicity of this was counteracted by the richness of its lace (Plate 41). New intricacies were devised for the ruff itself; hitherto it had been of one layer only, but now it was composed of two, or even three, tiers of pleating one above the other (Plate 50). The years from 1585 till 1600, indeed, display a great variety of different modes of neckwear, all fashionable at the same time. There is the loose, unstarched ruff of one tier, worn mostly just about the year 1590 (Plate 47); there is

11

the looser falling collar dividing almost horizontally from an open neck (Plate 48); and there is the curious complexity of wearing a falling collar under a ruff, to be seen for a time from 1595 onward (Plate 50). The ruffs of unmarried women were divided to reveal the bared bosom, and increased in depth as they receded (Plate 52).

In the reign of James I the whisk usurped the place of the ruff. This was derived from the falling collar by lifting it up and making it stand out at the back of the neck by means of a stiff support known as a 'pickadil'; hence the alternative name 'standing collar' for the whisk. Small and simple in 1605 (Plate 51), by 1610 the whisk had become a platform of exquisite lace and gave an appearance of John the Baptist's head on a charger to the person who wore it (Plate 49). But side by side with this fashion went a style in which women wore only a lace edging to the low-cut yoke of their bodices (Plate 53), and the formal pleated ruff of the 1580's was reintroduced (Plate 55). Saffron-coloured starch was introduced and was most popular for ruffs, bands, and lace in the period 1610–20. The inventor of this yellow starch was said to be Mrs Turner, and when that lady was executed in 1615 for complicity in the murder of Sir Thomas Overbury she, and her hangmen, wore yellow ruffs. The final stage of neckwear reached in the reign of James I was the falling band—embryonic in Plate 54, in its assured form by 1620 (Plate 56). The ruffle worn at the wrist corresponds with the neckwear up to at least the 1570's, but is latterly more often a turn-up cuff made of lace of greater or less elaboration.

Turning to the appearance of the costume as a whole, we can trace about half a dozen main types of silhouette in the entire Elizabethan and Jacobean Ages. The early Elizabethan style in female costume up to about 1570 has a rather pinched appearance, caused by the combination of tightly fitting sleeves with constricted bodices and wide skirts. In men's costume the same look of constriction is given by the combination of the tight sleeves and body of the doublet with the bulbous trunk hose; the doublet is, however, already of a slightly peascod shape.

In the 1570's and 1580's female costume becomes more elaborate and polychromatic, perhaps partly under the pressure of Queen Elizabeth's anxiety to enhance her fading charms. The large wings, large ruffs, and broadening leg-of-mutton sleeves enable the top of the costume to answer to the bell-shaped curves of the skirt; the material used becomes yet more colourful, and a greater profusion of jewels is apparent. Concurrently men's costume is at its most swaggering, and their jaunty feather-crowned caps, high collars, and long legs give them the air of game-cocks lording it over the barnyard, a suitable symbol of their masculinity.

By 1585, when the ruff had reached its greatest extent, Elizabethan female costume had attained its most pleasing aspect, with the wide leg-of-mutton sleeve, the slender bodice, and the bell of the skirt in harmonious relationship (Plates 14 and 15). At this time men's doublets acquired their furthest pitch of singularity, being provided with puffed sleeves comparable with those of the woman's bodice and the deep, drooping point of the full peascod belly which is preserved for us in the traditional garb

12

of Punch. But just at this time of greater formalism, and proceeding concurrently with it, a romantic reaction seems to have set in. As already recorded, young men began to wear the falling collar instead of the wide ruff, and their hair was arranged in curls which looked natural indeed. In the 1590's the doublet itself acquired a new looseness. It is hardly an accident that this Arcadian development coincided with the culminating period of Elizabethan sonnet-writing, Sidney's, Daniel's, Drayton's, Spenser's, and probably also Shakespeare's sequences all being written between 1585 and 1595.

The female answer to this turn in men's fashions was scarcely glamorous. In their late Elizabethan style the graceful bell skirt was converted into a drum, the bodice yet more restricted. It is hard not to suspect Queen Elizabeth of having driven the fashions of the last ten years of her reign into so perverse an extreme through a certain reckless-ness of her own appearance. But the delayed romanticism in female dress came about in the reign of James I. The old but psychologically improbable story that Queen Anne of Denmark wore out Queen Elizabeth's extensive left-over wardrobe finds no support in the portraits known of her, or in the uninterrupted movement of fashion. If she used up the fabrics of which they were made, she probably had them refashioned. At first the new line is visible in narrower farthingales and in the substitution of the whisk for the ruff, leaving scope for the *décolletage* of the bosom. Young women are por-trayed with their hair unloosed, and their garments have the same loose, flowing rhythm. The bodice is cut lower and the waist becomes higher. The male costume of the reign of James I preserves its recently acquired comfort; the doublet is less con-stricting and built to a normal waistline, and the hose hang full and loose. So the age of James I goes out on a note of relaxed tension, and prepares the ground for the familiar gallantry and picturesqueness of costume associated with the Cavaliers and the paintings of Van Dyck. But, though both that later stage of style and the obvious and undeniable charm of the eighteenth-century's modes are more popular and renowned, the instinct for clothes, and the sense of how to choose and wear them as an enhancement of the personality, was never at a higher level in England than in the Elizabethan and Jacobean period.

NOTES ON THE ILLUSTRATIONS

The majority of the portraits reproduced are inscribed with the date at which they were painted. Estimated dates, not supported by inscriptions on the portraits or other direct documentary evidence, have prefixed to them in these notes the abbreviation c. (for circa).

PLATE 1
1558

HANS EWORTH: *King Philip II of Spain and Queen Mary of England* (Duke of Bedford).
This plate illustrates the point of departure of the fashions of our period, for it dates from the year in which Mary Tudor died and Queen Elizabeth succeeded her. The Queen's dress of blue velvet is rich with brocade and fur, but severe and simple in comparison with the elaboration which Elizabeth was to foster; her skirt falls in a graceful Spanish farthingale, and the absence of any ruff is to be noted. King Philip is wearing a black jerkin over his pale-yellow doublet and hose; particularly to be remarked are the slashes in the jerkin to reveal the doublet, the long, hanging false sleeves, and the long skirts which almost cover his hose. The frill at his neck is the ruff in its smallest form, and was to grow to enormous proportions in the next thirty years.

PLATE 2
1559

HANS EWORTH: *Frances Brandon, Duchess of Suffolk, and Adrian Stoke, her Second Husband* (Private Collection).
The lady was herself close to the throne, and the magnificence of her attire is doubtless a survival of the ways of Henry VIII's Court rather than a reflection of Elizabeth's accession, as is the raked-back hair under her coif. Her ruffs and the ruffles at her wrists are edged with gold. Her husband wears a light-pink doublet beneath his furred coat, which is decorated with slashes and metal points.

PLATE 3
1561

ARTIST UNKNOWN: *Henry, Earl of Pembroke* (Duke of Leeds). (*Crown Copyright reserved.*)
This plate shows the male doublet and hose without the jerkin which conceals them in the costume of Philip II (Plate 1). The decoration is composed of simple vertical lines, the doublet is slightly but not exaggeratedly shaped, the hose are short, reaching barely half-way to the knee, and the codpiece is small. At this time the coat was often worn, as here, loosely over the shoulder, with the sleeves dangling in front. Notice the small flat cap, the high neck surmounted by a small ruff, and the heelless shoes following the natural form of the foot.

14

ANTONIO MORO: *Sir Henry Lee* (London, National Portrait Gallery). PLATE 4

The doublet is slashed vertically to show traces of the white shirt underneath. The 1568
neck is high and the ruff close-fitting under the chin. The armillary sphere and knot
patterns with which the shirt is decorated are doubtless of symbolic import. In the
dress of the sixteenth and seventeenth centuries rings are often shown as here, attached
to the person by cords.

ARTIST UNKNOWN: *Queen Elizabeth* (Hampden House, Earl of Buckinghamshire). PLATE 5

Not dated, but the small ruff, narrow sleeves, small 'wings,' and fairly natural bodice c. 1560–65
combine to place this portrait near the date of the Queen's accession. It is instructive
to compare the graceful silhouette with the frankly extravagant style adopted by the
Queen thirty years later (Plate 25). The *pointillé* decoration of the dress is particularly
effective.

ARTIST UNKNOWN: *An Unknown Girl, aged Eleven* (John Hanbury-Williams, Esq.). PLATE 6

This young lady's brocaded dress embodies the main features of the first decade of 1567
Elizabeth's reign—the bodice narrowing in a straight line to a point below the waist,
the farthingale swelling out like a bell below. Her sleeves are no doubt separable from
her dress and tied to it; the prominent 'wings' at the point where they join the shoulders,
and their method of decoration by puffs and panes, persist through the 1570's. The
band strings which could draw the ruff into a continuous circle round the neck are
seen hanging on the left.

HANS EWORTH: *Queen Elizabeth with Juno, Minerva, and Venus* (Hampton Court, PLATE 7
H.M. the King). (*Reproduced by gracious permission of His Majesty the King.*) 1569

This ingenious piece of Court flattery shows Queen Elizabeth overcoming the three
goddesses by her beauty. Her triumph is made easier because she is dressed in the
height of fashion. Her black-and-gold dress is of comparable form with that worn
in Plate 5, but the bodice tapers to a lower point, and she wears over it a robe or mantle
of which the train is borne by one of her ladies-in-waiting. The garment which Venus
has cast off, to the advantage of her charms, in the lower right-hand corner of the
picture, is of great interest: it is her shift or undergarment. It has a pattern embroidered
in green upon it, a ruff at the neck, and ruffles at the wrist.

JORIS HOEFNAGEL: *The Marriage Feast at Bermondsey* (Marquess of Salisbury). PLATE 8

This picture, which is signed by Hoefnagel, and must have been painted by him on 1568–69
his visit to England of 1568–69, gives a panorama of the costumes worn by the English
middle classes in the third quarter of the sixteenth century. The shapes of the clothes
of the more well-to-do are similar to those worn at Court at almost the same date
(Plates 4 and 7), but the fabrics used in them give the impression of being less rich and

more lasting. The women mostly wear gowns over their dresses and the men jerkins, or jerkins and cloaks, over their doublets. Notice the differences of padding and length in the hose worn by the men and the variety of headgear, in which the newer fashion is the bag-shaped bonnet with high crown.

PLATE 9 ARTIST UNKNOWN: *Sir Philip Sidney* (London, National Portrait Gallery).
1577   The white leather doublet is slashed vertically, and slightly peascod in shape. The full trunk hose are paned—*i.e.*, divided in vertical strips—and embroidered. The wearing of a gorget with civilian dress was a prerogative of military men. The codpiece is rarely seen so late in the century as this.

PLATE 10 STYLE OF GEORGE GOWER: *Called Lady Walsingham* (Lord de L'Isle and Dudley).
1572   The ruff has grown deeper and will now start to stand out farther and farther from the neck, till it reaches the extreme size of 1585 (Plate 17). The outer gown has gauze over-sleeves and 'wings' which are larger than those of the 1560's (Plates 5 and 7), and are, in fact, now almost at their extreme size. The gauze covering for the bosom between the top of the stomacher and bottom of the ruff was known as the 'partlet.'

PLATE 11 ARTIST UNKNOWN: *King James I of England, aged Eight* (London, National Portrait
1574 Gallery).
For the first time in these illustrations the breeches reach below the knee in the style known as 'Venetians'; they are padded very fully to give a well-rounded curve from the waist. The ornamental diagonal slashing on the shoes may be discerned.

PLATE 12 ARTIST UNKNOWN: *Sir Francis Drake* (Greenwich, National Maritime Museum).
1583   A companion picture to Plate 14, and, as a similar dated print of 1583 shows, contemporary with it. The falling lace collar or band in place of the ruff came into favour with some men in the 1580's, but the true decoration of such a collar is better understood from Plate 41. The peascod effect at the belly of the doublet, already pronounced in Plate 9, is greater here, and may be seen again in Plate 18. The sleeves of the doublet are puffed and wide, as in women's dress of the same period.

PLATE 13 ARTIST UNKNOWN (ENGLISH SCHOOL): *An Unknown Young Lady* (London, National
c. 1575–80 Portrait Gallery).
The full silhouette of this young lady would be intermediate between those of Plates 5 and 15. The large wings above her wide, loose sleeves, the partlet with a black design, and the complicated chains from which her jewellery is suspended are worthy of particular notice.

PLATE 14 ARTIST UNKNOWN: *Elizabeth, Second Wife of Sir Francis Drake* (Greenwich, National
1583 Maritime Museum).
This and Plate 12 are companion pictures. A certain loss of definition and form in the

16

details—for example, of the ruff and the lace collar—shows that these two pictures are old copies, probably of the eighteenth century; they are none the less valuable guides to the costume of the 1580's. The female silhouette is now composed of a constricted V-shaped bodice fitting into a widely spreading bell-shaped skirt. The sleeves have widened, and the ruff is not so high under the chin and is approaching its maximum diameter. At the wrist, in place of the ruffle, is a turn-up cuff edged with lace. The fan and the jewel pinned to the wide sleeve are now favourite accessories of costume. On the whole this and Plate 15 show Elizabethan female costume at its most attractive, before the exaggerated final phase set in.

NICHOLAS HILLIARD: *Called Anne Clifford, Countess of Pembroke* (Windsor, H.M. the King). (*Reproduced by gracious permission of His Majesty the King.*) PLATE 15 c. 1589

Not dated, but a head-and-shoulders miniature of the same lady dressed in the same style, in the collection of the Marquess of Anglesey, is dated 1589. Comparison with the full-length portrait of Elizabeth, Lady Drake (Plate 14), shows a similar silhouette, but with wider sleeves. The divided ruff which leaves the bosom uncovered is frequently from this time an indication that the lady is unmarried.

NICHOLAS HILLIARD: *An Unknown Lady* (London, Victoria and Albert Museum). PLATE 16 c. 1585

Undated, but not many years from the 'Ermine' Portrait of Queen Elizabeth (Plate 17). This invaluable drawing by the greatest Elizabethan artist shows the type of farthingale which was supported by an interior framework (known as the 'Spanish' farthingale) at its widest. The wings at the junction of sleeve and stomacher have shrunk to mere vestiges; in Plate 10 they are the most conspicuous part of the upper bodice, but here they are dwarfed by the wide sleeves. The six bows down each side are doubtless there to attach the changeable panel of embroidery to the remainder of the skirt. The hair is wired into the horn shape which is typical of women's coiffure in the 1570's and 1580's.

Attributed to NICHOLAS HILLIARD: *Queen Elizabeth* (Marquess of Salisbury). PLATE 17 1585

Known as the 'Ermine' Portrait of Queen Elizabeth, from the animal on her left arm which symbolizes her virginity, this shows the ruff verging on its greatest width, and composed of intricate lacework. The gauze veil behind the ruff is stiffened by wire to comprise 'hukes.' The dark dress, which is of the same form as those in Plates 14 and 15, is covered with a profusion of jewels and ornaments.

NICHOLAS HILLIARD: *An Unknown Young Man leaning against a Tree among Roses* (London, Victoria and Albert Museum). PLATE 18 c. 1588

Undated, but a head-and-shoulders miniature of the same youth at about the same age, in the Metropolitan Museum, New York, is dated 1588 (Plate 41). This elegant courtier wears trunk hose of the type shown in Plate 3, but abbreviated almost to disappearance to show the full symmetry of his legs. The doublet has a fully peascod belly, the sleeves are puffed, and the ruff is large, but not lacy. His black cloak is thrown over his left shoulder in the casual gesture with which this article was worn by Elizabethan gallants.

PLATE 19   ARTIST UNKNOWN: *Robert Dudley, Earl of Leicester* (Duke of Buccleuch).
c. 1588   Probably a seventeenth-century copy of a late sixteenth-century miniature. Undated, but the falling collar denotes that the Earl is displayed in the costume proper to the years near his death. The miniature is useful in showing the richly embroidered 'canions' (the closely fitting connexions between the very short breeches and the stockings) which were in vogue in the 1580's and 1590's. Compare the hanging peascod belly with that in Plate 12. The short cloak, doublet, breeches, canions, and stockings all bear different designs.

PLATE 20   ISAAC OLIVER: *A Young Man* (formerly called *Sir Philip Sidney*) (Windsor, H.M. the
c. 1595   King). (*Reproduced by gracious permission of His Majesty the King.*)
          This plate is incidentally an illustration of the value of the study of costume in correcting historical misconception, for it has long passed as a portrait of Sir Philip Sidney, who died in 1586, aged thirty-four. The miniature certainly symbolizes our idea of the romantic and gallant poet, but the loosely falling collar, loose doublet, and abbreviated hose of the young man, and the minute figures in the right distance—the woman is wearing a skirt well above her ankles—all point to a date in the 1590's.

PLATE 21   MARCUS GHEERAERTS: *Lady Sidney and her Children* (Lord de L'Isle and Dudley).
1596   This charming group is especially instructive in showing how children of different sexes and ages were dressed. The basic lines are between those of the Ditchley Queen Elizabeth (Plate 25) and the Blackfriars Wedding (Plate 24), but provide for some individual variation. The mother rests her hands on the two boys of the family, and the remaining four children are girls. It will be noticed that the elder boy is quite literally in skirts, and that, like his sisters, he wears a farthingale.

PLATE 22   ISAAC OLIVER: *The Three Brothers Browne and their Page* (Marquess of Exeter).
1598   Looseness has once again come into male attire, in the fit of the doublet and hose and in the hang of the collars. It must have been welcome after the high ruffs and constricted doublets of the previous decades. The page on the right has his cloak loosely round him, and his ruff, of which the detail is obscured in the reproduction, is of the three-layer type shown in Plate 50.

PLATE 23   ARTIST UNKNOWN: *Mary Fitton* (The Hon. Mrs Fitzroy Newdegate).
c. 1600   Undated, but wearing a notably bizarre version of the costume in evidence at the Blackfriars Wedding (Plate 24). The false sleeves have edges reminiscent of a coxcomb's cap, and the pale-brown skirt is embroidered with insects. The locket suspended at her bosom doubtless opens to reveal a miniature.

18

Attributed to MARCUS GHEERAERTS: *Queen Elizabeth's Visit to Blackfriars for the* PLATE 24
Marriage of Henry, Lord Herbert, with Anne Russell (Colonel F. J. B. Wingfield 1600
Digby).

This represents an assembly of the most important courtiers at the end of Queen
Elizabeth's reign, and illustrates the variety possible under the apparent uniformity
of courtly dress. The Queen herself, strangely rejuvenated, is shown in a dress on much
the same lines as that she wore at Ditchley eight years before (Plate 25). Among the
ladies on the right, the married have ruffs of a complete circle, and their bosoms are
covered, while the unmarried leave the top of the bosom bare. Notice the coiffure
rising well off the head at the back. Two main types of ruff are in favour among the
men—the triple-layered (as Plate 50) and the single-layered with large organ pleats,
but a falling band and other varieties are to be discerned. Notice the way of wearing
cloaks and the method of suspension of the swords.

ARTIST UNKNOWN: *Queen Elizabeth* (London, National Portrait Gallery). PLATE 25
This picture was painted to commemorate the visit of Queen Elizabeth to Ditchley in 1592
1592. She is wearing the costume of the last phase of her reign, with all its exaggera-
tions at their most extreme—the narrow, conical bodice fitting into an enormous
drum farthingale, and the leg-of-mutton sleeves framed by false sleeves which reach
to the ground. Apart from the cord of her fan, the only colour on the Queen's
dress is provided by the jewels with which it is lavishly covered. The folding fan has
replaced the former type illustrated in Plate 16.

Attributed to PAUL VAN SOMER: *Called Lady Arabella Stuart* (Duke of Bedford). PLATE 26
In similar costume to the preceding lady, but the headdress is piled higher and to the c. 1600–05
front, with rich jewellery, and the hair falls loosely from it on either side.

E. M.: *Lettice Newdegate, aged Two* (The Hon. Mrs Fitzroy Newdegate). PLATE 27
This little girl wears the rising band of the time, and her bodice and skirt falling 1606
without excessive farthingale foreshadow a coming simplicity of outline, seen fully
developed in Plate 34.

ARTIST UNKNOWN: *An Unknown Lady* (The Hon. Michael Astor). PLATE 28
Exemplifies the delight taken, particularly in the early years of the seventeenth 1607
century, in decoration by lavish embroidery in the circular coiling stem pattern, and
of its combination with lace and gauze. Notice that the farthingale is less full and
shaped off the hips by a roll, not a hoop.

ARTIST UNKNOWN: *Anne Vavasour* (Francis Howard, Esq.). PLATE 29
Undated, but the standing ruff and high coiffure indicate a date of c. 1600–5. c. 1600–05
The drum farthingale is not so wide as in the costume worn by Queen Elizabeth at

Ditchley (Plate 25), and is slightly shorter in length, revealing the bottom of the shift below. Note that the shoes have spatulate toes and no heels.

PLATE 30 PAUL VAN SOMER: *Queen Anne of Denmark* (Duke of Bedford).
c. 1610   Undated, but the standing band and wide drum farthingale refer it to the first decade of the reign of James I. The leg-of-mutton sleeves have disappeared, and the false sleeves have shrunk to a vestigial strip of material. The low circular top of the bodice, and its edging of lace, is a common feature in the costume of this time, and married, no less than single, women may now leave the bosom uncovered. The 'S' suspended from her whisk was one of Queen Anne's favourite jewels; it denotes the initial of her mother, Sophia of Mecklenburg.

PLATE 31 ARTIST UNKNOWN (DUTCH SCHOOL): *Phineas Pett* (London, National Portrait Gallery).
1613   The professional man—he was Master Builder of the Navy—wears a simple and practical costume, but his 'night cap' is a good specimen of English embroidery. The 'night cap' was worn indoors, but not in bed.

PLATE 32 ROBERT PEAKE: *Prince Charles I* (The University of Cambridge).
1613   In this fine specimen of Court dress Prince Charles wears a large whisk collar, an embroidered doublet, and full pleated breeches. A cloak is thrown over his left shoulder, and his hat, on the table, has a high crown.

PLATE 33 ISAAC OLIVER: *Richard Sackville, Third Earl of Dorset* (London, Victoria and Albert
1616 Museum).
    The costume of a man described as a "licentious spendthrift." The doublet and the sleeves fit the body naturally. He wears a lace whisk, or standing ruff (cf. Plate 49), and cuffs. The paned trunk hose hang fully, and show the inner lining. The sun, moon, and stars embroidered on them reflect the delight in symbolism and emblems inherited by the Jacobean from the Elizabethan Age. The embroidered clocks on the stockings (and on the tablecloth) are similar in pattern to the decorations of the skirt in Plate 37. The shoe has now a heel, and rosettes at their buckles are now in favour.

PLATE 34 Attributed to DANIEL MYTENS: *Anne, Countess of Stamford* (Margaret, Countess of
c. 1615 Suffolk and Berkshire).

PLATE 35 Attributed to DANIEL MYTENS: *Catherine, Countess of Suffolk* (Margaret, Countess
c. 1615 of Suffolk and Berkshire).
    A great deal of the artist's feeling for fabrics has entered into these two delightful representations of costume. A new variety and style of design, a new sophistication,

20

are apparent in the decorations of the bodices and skirts and the lacework of the ruffs and turned-back cuffs. The skirts fall from a padding at the hips without framework; that of the Countess of Suffolk retains still the pleats which were developed at the top of the drum farthingale (Plates 23 and 30), but they are now vestigial. The large and costly handkerchief is a frequent accessory in portraits of this period. It will be seen that the shoe has now a well-defined heel.

DANIEL MYTENS: *James Hamilton, Second Marquess of Hamilton* (Windsor, H.M. the King). (*Reproduced by gracious permission of His Majesty the King.*) PLATE 36
1624–25

The inscription states that the portrait was painted in 1622, but is presumed to have been repainted with an error, since the sitter did not become Lord Steward, the staff of which office he bears, till 1624. In any case this painting shows the Jacobean passing over into the Cavalier styles familiar in the paintings of Van Dyck. The points which formerly were used for tying the breeches to the stockings have become a vestigial hanging fringe. The long, closely fitting boots turned down to below the knee were to become a familiar sight in the reign of Charles I.

MARCUS GHEERAERTS: *Elizabeth Cherry, Lady Russell* (Duke of Bedford). PLATE 37

In this portrait, painted in the year King James I died, female dress foreshadows the 1625
higher waistline and freely hanging skirt associated with the era when Van Dyck worked in England. A gauze apron covers the full embroidered skirt, and an overrobe is worn over the bodice and fastened at the shoulders.

PAUL VAN SOMER: *Queen Anne of Denmark with her Dogs* (Windsor, H.M. the King). PLATE 38
(*Reproduced by gracious permission of His Majesty the King.*) 1617

Representative of the lines of female costume in the middle of the reign of King James I, and of its preference for subdued colouring. The farthingale has been reduced to a padding round the hips from which the full skirt falls in natural folds; the bosom is cut low in a circular yoke. The lace of the ruff and the cuffs and round the yoke of the bodice is dyed with saffron.

[*Notes on Plates 39–56 begin on page 22.*]

1577–1620 RUFFS AND COIFFURES

PL. 39, 1577   NICHOLAS HILLIARD: *Portrait of the Artist* (London, Victoria and Albert Museum).

PL. 40, 1585   NICHOLAS HILLIARD: *Sir Francis Knowles* (Duke of Buccleuch).

PL. 41, 1588   NICHOLAS HILLIARD: *An Unknown Youth* (New York, Metropolitan Museum).

PL. 42, 1578   NICHOLAS HILLIARD: *Alice Hilliard* (London, Victoria and Albert Museum).

PL. 43, c. 1585   NICHOLAS HILLIARD: *An Unknown Lady* (Duke of Buccleuch).

PL. 44, c. 1585   NICHOLAS HILLIARD: *An Unknown Lady* (Earl of Radnor).

PL. 45, c. 1590   ISAAC OLIVER: *An Unknown Lady* (Amsterdam, Rijksmuseum).

PL. 46, 1593   NICHOLAS HILLIARD: *Mrs Holland* (London, Victoria and Albert Museum).

PL. 47, 1590   ISAAC OLIVER: *An Unknown Man* (London, Victoria and Albert Museum).

PL. 48, 1597   NICHOLAS HILLIARD: *An Unknown Man* (London, Victoria and Albert Museum).

PL. 49, 1610   ISAAC OLIVER: *An Unknown Man* (London, Victoria and Albert Museum).

PL. 50, 1599   SCHOOL OF NICHOLAS HILLIARD: *An Unknown Man* (Duke of Buccleuch).

PL. 51, 1605   NICHOLAS HILLIARD: *An Unknown Lady* (Marquess of Salisbury).

PL. 52, 1600   (Detail from the lower right-hand corner of Plate 24.)

PL. 53, c. 1610   ISAAC OLIVER: *Lady Arabella Stuart* (Amsterdam, Rijksmuseum).

PL. 54, c. 1615   PETER OLIVER: *A Lady*, perhaps *Venetia Digby* (Viscount Bearsted).

PL. 55, c. 1610   ISAAC OLIVER: *Henry Frederick, Prince of Wales* (Windsor, H.M. the King).
(*Reproduced by gracious permission of His Majesty the King.*)

PL. 56, 1620   CORNELIUS JOHNSON: *An Unknown Man* (Bath, Holburne of Menstrie Museum).

22

The earlier plates have shown in broad outline the development of hair styles and also of that most changeable element in Elizabethan and Jacobean costume, the ruff or neck-band. Plates 39–56 fill in some of the details of these variations. Plates 39 and 42 show the ruff beginning to stand out widely, from a high neck, and Plates 40, 43, and 44 show the 'cartwheel' ruff at its most enormous, and the inexhaustible variety of lace designs which went to the most expensive bands. Plate 41 shows one of the loveliest of the falling bands which became fashionable with men c. 1585–90. Plate 45 shows a plain, wide ruff of one layer; Plate 46 a ruff of two layers, wider towards the back, a form which was worn in the last decade of Elizabeth's reign. The women on this page are wearing forms of horned hair style. Mrs Hilliard (Plate 42) has a black French hood falling behind her ruff; the lady in Plate 44 appears to be wearing a coif.

The man in Plate 47 is wearing a loose ruff, as though it were of the form of Plate 45, but unstarched, a style which is only seen c. 1590. The falling band of Plate 48 is different from that of the 1580's (Plate 41) in falling more widely apart; with it the doublet is worn open at the top. Plate 52 illustrates the ruffs which form a complete circle, (on the extreme right and left) as worn by married women, whereas those leaving the bosom uncovered indicate that the wearers are unmarried. The horned hair style has given way to one rising off the forehead and surmounted by jewels. Plate 50 shows the same falling band as in Plate 48, worn under a ruff of three layers; both the latter and the practice of wearing two neckbands at the same time are characteristic of the years c. 1595–1600. Plate 51 illustrates the rising neckband or whisk—the wired pickadil which supports it can be seen underneath it—and the round-cut *décolleté* bosom edged with lace, which were the first new styles in the reign of King James I.

Plate 49 shows the whisk of Plate 51 in its most developed and ornamental form; it is this style, in a more simple example, that Shakespeare wears in the Droeshout portrait. Plate 53 illustrates the charming Jacobean fashion of unloosed hair, and Plate 54 marks the birth of the new falling band whose definitive form is seen in Plate 56. Notice the embroidered bodices and the progressive *décolletage* in Plates 53 and 54. Plate 56 shows the final neck style of the Jacobean period.

SHORT BIBLIOGRAPHY

P. Macquoid: "Costume," vol. ii, Chapter XIX, of *Shakespeare's England* (Clarendon Press, Oxford, 1916).

F. M. Kelly: "Shakespearian Dress Notes," *Burlington Magazine*, vol. xxix (1916), pp. 91–98, 245–250, and 357–363.

F. M. Kelly and R. Schwabe: *Historic Costume, 1490–1790* (Batsford, London; second edition, 1929).

F. M. Kelly and R. Schwabe: *A Short History of Costume and Armour* (Batsford, London, 1931).

M. C. Linthicum: *Costume in the Drama of Shakespeare and his Contemporaries* (Clarendon Press, Oxford, 1936).

J. L. Nevinson: "English Embroidered Costume; Elizabethan and James I," *Connoisseur*, vol. xcvii (1936), pp. 23–28 and 140–144.

F. M. Kelly: *Shakespearian Costume for Stage and Screen* (A. and C. Black, London, 1938).

F. M. Kelly: "Queen Elizabeth and her Dresses," *Connoisseur*, vol. cxiii (1944), pp. 71–79.

ACKNOWLEDGMENT

The author wishes to thank all those who have kindly given permission for paintings to be reproduced in this monograph.

G.R.

Victoria and Albert Museum, London

Plate 1   Hans Eworth   1558

Plate 2   Hans Eworth   1559

Plate 3   Artist Unknown   1561

Plate 4   Antonio Moro   1568

Plate 5   Artist Unknown   c. 1560-65

ANNO·DOMINI·1567 ·ET·ANNO ÆTATIS·SVÆ·II·

Plate 6   Artist Unknown   1567

Plate 7

Hans Eworth

1569

1568-69

Joris Hoefnagel

Plate 8

Plate 9   Artist Unknown   1577

AN° DÑI 1572

ÆTATIS SVÆ 22

Plate 10   Style of George Gower   1572

Plate 11   Artist Unknown   1574

Plate 12   Artist Unknown   1583

Plate 13 Artist Unknown (English School) c. 1575-80

Plate 14   Artist Unknown   1583

Plate 15   Nicholas Hilliard   c. 1589

Plate 16   Nicholas Hilliard   c. 1585

Plate 17   Attributed to Nicholas Hilliard   1585

Plate 18   Nicholas Hilliard   c. 1588

ROBERT DUDLEY Erle
of Leicester, late Steward of
houshold to Queene Elizabeth,
for his singuler gyfts of the
mynde, & graces of his person
was aduaunced, honored, and
followed more then others.
He dyed the 2.. yeare of his
age, Anno. 1588

Plate 19   Artist Unknown   c. 1588

Plate 20   Isaac Oliver   c. 1595

Marcus Gheeraerts

Plate 21

Plate 22

Isaac Oliver

1598

Plate 23   Artist Unknown   c. 1600

Plate 24

Attributed to Marcus Gheeraerts

1600

Plate 25   Artist Unknown   1592

Plate 26   Attributed to Paul van Somer   c. 1600-05

Plate 27   E.M.   1606

Plate 28   Artist Unknown   1607

Plate 29   Artist Unknown   c. 1600-05

Plate 30　　　　　　　　Paul van Somer　　　　　　　c. 1610

ÆTAT SVÆ 43.

Plate 31   Artist Unknown (Dutch School)   1613

Plate 32   Robert Peake   1613

Plate 33   Isaac Oliver   1616

Plate 34   Attributed to Daniel Mytens   c. 1615

Plate 35   Attributed to Daniel Mytens   c. 1615

Plate 36   Daniel Mytens   1624-25

Plate 37   Marcus Gheeraerts   1625

Plate 38   Paul van Somer   1617

39 [1577]

40 [1585]

41 [1588]

42 [1578]

43 [c. 1585]

44 [c. 1585]

45 [c. 1590]

46 [1593]

39-44, 46   Nicholas Hilliard   45   Isaac Oliver

47 [1590]   48 [1597]

49 [1610]

50 [1599]   51 [1605]

47, 49   Isaac Oliver   48, 51   Nicholas Hilliard   50   School of Nicholas Hilliard

Plate 52   Detail from Plate 24   1600

53 [c. 1610]　　　　　　　　　　　　54 [c. 1615]

53　Isaac Oliver　　　　　　　　　54　Peter Oliver

Plate 55　　　Isaac Oliver　　　c. 1610　　　Plate 56　　　Cornelius Johnson　　　1620